Table of Contents

The Original Rice Krispies® Treats

PREP TIME: 10 minutes ■ **TOTAL TIME: 10 minutes**

Makes 12 servings

> 3 tablespoons margarine or butter
> 4 cups miniature marshmallows or 1 package (10 ounces, about 40) regular marshmallows
> 6 cups *Kellogg's® Rice Krispies®* Cereal

1. Melt margarine in large saucepan over low heat. Add marshmallows and stir until completely melted. Remove from heat.

2. Add KELLOGG'S RICE KRISPIES cereal. Stir until well coated.

3. Using buttered spatula or waxed paper, press mixture evenly into 13×9×2-inch pan coated with cooking spray. Cut into 2-inch squares when cool. Best if served the same day. Store no more than two days in airtight container.

MICROWAVE DIRECTIONS: In a microwave safe bowl, heat margarine and marshmallows at HIGH 3 minutes, stirring after 2 minutes. Stir until smooth. Follow steps 2 and 3 above. Microwave cooking times may vary.

NOTES: For best results, use fresh marshmallows. 1 jar (7 ounces) marshmallow crème can be substituted for marshmallows. Diet, reduced-calorie or tub margarine is not recommended.

Fun Balls

PREP TIME: 40 minutes ▪ **TOTAL TIME: 40 minutes**

Makes 12 servings

> 3 tablespoons margarine or butter
>
> 4 cups miniature marshmallows or 1 package (10 ounces, about 40) regular marshmallows
>
> 6 cups *Kellogg's® Rice Krispies®* Cereal or *Kellogg's® Cocoa Krispies®* Cereal
>
> 12 wooden ice cream sticks
>
> Flaked coconut (optional)
>
> Semi-sweet chocolate chips, melted (optional)
>
> Decorator sprinkles (optional)

1. Melt margarine in large saucepan over low heat. Add marshmallows and stir until completely melted. Remove from heat.

2. Add KELLOGG'S RICE KRISPIES cereal. Stir until well coated.

3. Using ½ cup measure coated with cooking spray, portion hot cereal mixture. Shape into balls, inserting wooden stick. Roll and press in coconut or drizzle with chocolate. Faces can be created with frosting, marshmallows or candies, if desired. Best if served the same day. Store no more than two days in airtight container.

MICROWAVE DIRECTIONS: In a microwave safe bowl, heat margarine and marshmallows at HIGH 3 minutes, stirring after 2 minutes. Stir until smooth. Follow steps 2 and 3 above. Microwave cooking times may vary.

NOTES: For best results, use fresh marshmallows. 1 jar (7 ounces) marshmallow crème can be substituted for marshmallows. Diet, reduced-calorie or tub margarine is not recommended.

Birthday Fun Cups

PREP TIME: **40 minutes**   ▥   TOTAL TIME: **40 minutes**

Makes 12 servings

> 3 **tablespoons margarine or butter**
> 4 **cups miniature marshmallows or 1 package (10 ounces, about 40) regular marshmallows**
> 6 **cups** *Kellogg's® Rice Krispies®* **Cereal or** *Kellogg's® Cocoa Krispies®* **Cereal**
> **Pudding, ice cream or frozen yogurt**

1. Melt margarine in large saucepan over low heat. Add marshmallows and stir until completely melted. Remove from heat.

2. Add KELLOGG'S RICE KRISPIES cereal. Stir until well coated.

3. Divide warm mixture into 2½-inch muffin-pan cups coated with cooking spray. Shape mixture into individual cups. Cool. Remove from pans. Just before serving, fill with pudding, ice cream or frozen yogurt. Serve immediately. Store no more than two days in airtight container.

MICROWAVE DIRECTIONS: In a microwave safe bowl, heat margarine and marshmallows at HIGH 3 minutes, stirring after 2 minutes. Stir until smooth. Follow steps 2 and 3 above. Microwave cooking times may vary.

NOTES: For best results, use fresh marshmallows. 1 jar (7 ounces) marshmallow crème can be substituted for marshmallows. Diet, reduced-calorie or tub margarine is not recommended.

Pizza Treats

PREP TIME: 15 minutes ▓ **TOTAL TIME: 35 minutes**

Makes 12 servings

3 **tablespoons butter or margarine**

1 **package (10 ounces, about 40) regular marshmallows
   or 4 cups miniature marshmallows**

6 **cups _Kellogg's® Rice Krispies®_ Cereal or 6 cups
   Kellogg's® Cocoa Krispies® Cereal**

Strawberry jam

Canned frosting

Fruit roll-ups, cut into 1¼-inch circles

Multi-colored sprinkles

1. In large saucepan, melt butter over low heat. Add marshmallows and stir until completely melted. Remove from heat.

2. Add KELLOGG'S RICE KRISPIES cereal. Stir until well coated.

3. Using buttered spatula or wax paper, evenly press mixture into 12-inch pizza pan coated with cooking spray. Cool.

4. Spread strawberry jam on top for "tomato sauce". Carefully spread frosting over jam for "cheese". Add fruit roll-up circles for "pepperoni". Top with sprinkles. Cut into slices to serve. Best if served the same day.

MICROWAVE DIRECTIONS: In a microwave safe bowl, heat butter and marshmallows at HIGH 3 minutes, stirring after 2 minutes. Stir until smooth. Follow steps 2 and 4 above. Microwave cooking times may vary.

NOTES: For best results, use fresh marshmallows. 1 jar (7 ounces) marshmallow crème can be substituted for marshmallows. Diet, reduced-calorie or tub margarine is not recommended. Stir no more than two days at room temperature in airtight container. To freeze, place in single layer on wax paper in airtight container. Freeze for up to 6 weeks. Let stand at room temperature for 15 minutes before serving.

Chocolate Scotcheroos

PREP TIME: 20 minutes ▥ **TOTAL TIME: 1 hour 20 minutes**

Makes 24 servings

> 1 **cup light corn syrup**
> 1 **cup sugar**
> 1 **cup creamy peanut butter**
> 6 **cups *Kellogg's® Rice Krispies® Cereal or Kellogg's® Cocoa Krispies® Cereal***
> 1 **cup semi-sweet chocolate chips (6 ounces)**
> 1 **cup butterscotch chips**

1. Place corn syrup and sugar into 3-quart saucepan. Cook over medium heat, stirring frequently, until sugar dissolves and mixture begins to boil. Remove from heat. Stir in peanut butter. Mix well. Add KELLOGG'S RICE KRISPIES cereal. Stir until well coated. Press mixture into 13×9×2-inch pan coated with cooking spray. Set aside.

2. Melt chocolate and butterscotch chips together in 1-quart saucepan over low heat, stirring constantly. Spread evenly over cereal mixture. Let stand until firm. Cut into 2×1-inch bars when cool.

Peanut Butter Bars

PREP TIME: 20 minutes ▥ **TOTAL TIME: 1 hour**

Makes 12 servings

> 1 **cup reduced-fat creamy peanut butter**
> 3 **tablespoons margarine, softened**
> 1 **cup powdered sugar**
> 3 **cups *Kellogg's® Rice Krispies® Cereal* or *Kellogg's® Cocoa Krispies® Cereal***
> ¼ **cup melted semi-sweet chocolate chips**
> **Decorator sprinkles (optional)**

1. In large mixer bowl, combine peanut butter, margarine and powdered sugar on medium speed. Add KELLOGG'S RICE KRISPIES cereal, mixing until thoroughly combined. Press mixture evenly into 9×9×2-inch pan coated with cooking spray. Refrigerate until firm.

2. Drizzle chocolate over cereal mixture. Decorate with sprinkles, if desired. Refrigerate about 30 minutes or until chocolate is set and cereal mixture is firm. Cut into 2×1½-inch bars. Store in airtight container in refrigerator.

Rice Krispies® Brownies

PREP TIME: 15 minutes ■ **TOTAL TIME: 1 hour 30 minutes**

Makes 24 servings

> 3 cups *Kellogg's® Rice Krispies®* Cereal, crushed to ¾ cup
>
> 2 cups sugar
>
> ½ cup all-purpose flour
>
> ½ cup unsweetened baking cocoa powder
>
> ¼ teaspoon salt
>
> ½ cup chopped pecans
>
> ½ cup vegetable oil
>
> 3 eggs, slightly beaten
>
> ¼ cup non-fat milk
>
> 1 teaspoon vanilla extract

1. In large mixing bowl, combine KELLOGG'S RICE KRISPIES cereal, sugar, flour, cocoa powder, salt and pecans. Add remaining ingredients and mix only until combined. Spread evenly in 13×9×2-inch baking pan coated with cooking spray.

2. Bake at 350°F about 30 minutes or until wooden pick inserted at center comes out clean. Cool completely on wire rack before cutting into 2-inch squares. Store tightly covered at room temperature.

Cocoa Krispies® Treats

PREP TIME: 10 minutes ■ **TOTAL TIME: 30 minutes**

Makes 12 servings

3 tablespoons butter or margarine

1 package (10 ounces, about 40) regular marshmallows or 4 cups miniature marshmallows

6 cups *Kellogg's® Cocoa Krispies®* Cereal

1. In large saucepan, melt butter over low heat. Add marshmallows and stir until completely melted. Remove from heat.

2. Add KELLOGG'S COCOA KRISPIES cereal. Stir until well coated.

3. Using buttered spatula or wax paper, evenly press mixture into 13×9×2-inch pan coated with cooking spray. Cool. Cut into 2-inch squares. Best if served the same day.

MICROWAVE DIRECTIONS: In microwave-safe bowl, heat butter and marshmallows on HIGH for 3 minutes, stirring after 2 minutes. Stir until smooth. Follow steps 2 and 3 above. Microwave cooking times may vary.

NOTES: For best results, use fresh marshmallows. 1 jar (7 ounces) marshmallow crème can be substituted for marshmallows. Diet, reduced-calorie or tub margarine is not recommended. Store no more than two days at room temperature in airtight container. To freeze, place in layers separated by wax paper in airtight container. Freeze for up to 6 weeks. Let stand at room temperature for 15 minutes before serving.

Peanut Butter Treats

PREP TIME: 10 minutes ■ **TOTAL TIME: 20 minutes**

Makes 12 servings

> 3 **tablespoons butter or margarine**
> 1 **package (10 ounces, about 40) regular marshmallows or 4 cups miniature marshmallows**
> ½ **cup peanut butter**
> 6 **cups *Kellogg's® Rice Krispies® Cereal***

1. In large saucepan, melt butter over low heat. Add marshmallows and stir until completely melted. Remove from heat. Stir in peanut butter until melted.

2. Add KELLOGG'S RICE KRISPIES cereal. Stir until well coated.

3. Using buttered spatula or wax paper, evenly press mixture into 13×9×2-inch pan coated with cooking spray. Cool. Cut into 2-inch squares. Best if served the same day.

MICROWAVE DIRECTIONS: In microwave-safe bowl, heat butter and marshmallows on HIGH for 3 minutes, stirring after 2 minutes. Stir until smooth. Add peanut butter, stirring until combined. Follow steps 2 and 3 above. Microwave cooking times may vary.

NOTES: For best results, use fresh marshmallows. 1 jar (7 ounces) marshmallow crème can be substituted for marshmallows. Diet, reduced-calorie or tub margarine is not recommended. Store no more than two days at room temperature in airtight container. To freeze, place in layers separated by wax paper in airtight container. Freeze for up to 6 weeks. Let stand at room temperature for 15 minutes before serving.

Neapolitan Treats

PREP TIME: 20 minutes ▦ **TOTAL TIME: 1 hour 20 minutes**

Makes 10 servings

1½ **cups strawberry ice cream, softened**
1½ **cups chocolate ice cream, softened**
3 **tablespoons butter or margarine**
1 **package (10 ounces, about 40) regular marshmallows or 4 cups miniature marshmallows**
6 **cups** *Kellogg's® Rice Krispies®* **Cereal**

1. Wash and dry two 12-ounce frozen juice concentrate cans. Pack strawberry ice cream into one can. Pack chocolate ice cream into other can. Cover and freeze at least 2 hours or until firm.*

2. Meanwhile, in large saucepan melt butter over low heat. Add marshmallows and stir until completely melted. Remove from heat.

3. Add KELLOGG'S RICE KRISPIES cereal. Stir until well coated.

4. Using buttered spatula or wax paper, evenly press mixture into 13×9×2-inch pan coated with cooking spray. Cool slightly. Using cookie cutter coated with cooking spray cut into ten 2½-inch circles.

5. Remove ice cream from freezer. Cut or tear paper sides of cans from ice cream. Cut ice cream cylinders into ten slices. In each dessert dish place one slice of strawberry ice cream, one KELLOGG'S RICE KRISPIES TREAT bar and one slice of chocolate ice cream. Serve immediately.**

If desired, omit packing ice cream into frozen juice concentrate cans. Prepare Kellogg's® Rice Krispies® Treats as directed above.

**To serve, in each dessert dish, place one small scoop of strawberry ice cream, one Kellogg's® Rice Krispies® Treat and one small scoop of chocolate ice cream. Serve immediately.*

NOTES: For best results, use fresh marshmallows. 1 jar (7 ounces) marshmallow crème can be substituted for marshmallows. Diet, reduced-calorie or tub margarine is not recommended.

Upside-Down Confetti Treats

PREP TIME: 10 minutes ▌ **TOTAL TIME: 30 minutes**

Makes 12 servings

½ **cup miniature candy-coated semi-sweet chocolate pieces**

3 **tablespoons butter or margarine**

1 **package (10 ounces, about 40) regular marshmallows or 4 cups miniature marshmallows**

6 **cups** *Kellogg's® Rice Krispies®* **Cereal**

1. Coat 13×9×2-inch pan with cooking spray. Evenly sprinkle candy on bottom of pan. Set aside.

2. In large saucepan, melt butter over low heat. Add marshmallows and stir until completely melted. Remove from heat.

3. Add KELLOGG'S RICE KRISPIES cereal. Stir until well coated.

4. Using buttered spatula or wax paper, evenly press mixture over candy in pan. Cool. Cut into 2-inch squares. Serve candy-side up. Best if served the same day.

Chocolate Yummies

PREP TIME: 20 minutes   ■   **TOTAL TIME: 1 hour 20 minutes**

Makes 36 servings

> 7 sheets *Keebler*® **Original Graham Crackers***
> 2½ cups miniature marshmallows
> 2 cups semi-sweet chocolate chips (12 ounces)
> ⅔ cup light corn syrup
> 3 tablespoons butter or margarine
> ½ cup chunky peanut butter
> 3 cups *Kellogg's*® *Rice Krispies*® **Cereal**
>
> **Each cracker sheet measures about 5×2-inches and is scored into 4 pieces.*

1. Coat 13×9×2-inch microwave-safe dish with cooking spray. Arrange KEEBLER GRAHAM crackers in a single layer over bottom of dish, breaking crackers as needed to fit. Sprinkle marshmallows evenly over crackers.

2. Microwave on HIGH 1 minute or until marshmallows are puffy. Remove from microwave. Cool completely.

3. In 2-quart microwave safe mixing bowl, combine chocolate chips, corn syrup and butter. Microwave on HIGH about 1½ minutes or until chocolate is melted, stirring every 30 seconds. Stir in peanut butter. Add KELLOGG'S RICE KRISPIES cereal, mixing until combined.

4. Spread mixture evenly over marshmallows. Cover and refrigerate about 1 hour or until firm. Cut and store in airtight container in refrigerator.

CONVENTIONAL DIRECTIONS: Follow step 1 above using 13×9×2-inch baking dish coated with cooking spray. Bake at 375°F about 7 minutes or until marshmallows are puffy. Cool completely. In medium saucepan, combine chocolate chips, corn syrup and butter. Cook stirring constantly, over medium-low heat until melted. Remove from heat. Stir in peanut butter. Add cereal, mixing until combined.

Peanut Butter and Jelly Crisps

PREP TIME: 20 minutes   ▥   **TOTAL TIME: 1 hour**

Makes 18 servings

- ¼ **cup margarine or butter**
- 1 **package (10 ounces, about 40) regular marshmallows or 4 cups miniature marshmallows**
- ¼ **cup creamy peanut butter**
- 5 **cups *Kellogg's® Rice Krispies®* Cereal**
- ⅓ **cup mixed fruit jelly**

1. Melt margarine in large saucepan over low heat. Add marshmallows and stir until completely melted. Cook over low heat 3 minutes longer, stirring constantly. Stir in peanut butter. Remove from heat.

2. Add KELLOGG'S RICE KRISPIES cereal. Stir until well coated.

3. Using buttered spatula or waxed paper, press half the mixture evenly into 9-inch square pan coated with cooking spray. Spread with jelly. Top with remaining cereal mixture, pressing gently. Chill until firm. Cut into 1½-inch squares. Best if served the same day. Store no more than two days in airtight container.

NOTES: For best results, use fresh marshmallows. 1 jar (7 ounces) marshmallow crème can be substituted for marshmallows. Diet, reduced-calorie or tub margarine is not recommended.

Chocolate Peanut Butter Balls

PREP TIME: 40 minutes ■ **TOTAL TIME: 1 hour 40 minutes**

Makes 27 servings

1	cup chunky peanut butter
¼	cup margarine or butter, softened
1	cup powdered sugar
2	cups *Kellogg's® Rice Krispies® Cereal*
54	mini-muffin paper cups
1½	cups semi-sweet chocolate chips
2	tablespoons vegetable shortening

1. In large electric mixer bowl, beat peanut butter, margarine and powdered sugar on medium speed until thoroughly combined. Add KELLOGG'S RICE KRISPIES cereal, mixing thoroughly. Portion mixture, using rounded teaspoon. Shape into balls. Place each ball in paper cup. Refrigerate.

2. Melt chocolate chips and shortening in small saucepan, over low heat, stirring constantly. Spoon 1 teaspoon melted chocolate over each peanut butter ball. Refrigerate until firm. Store in airtight container in refrigerator.